U0056736

# Walking Meditation

...ars wide open, I slowly lift my foot; gently moving
...orward, I place it on the ground, fully aware all the while.

...esearch and Publication Center
...f Ling Jiou Mountain

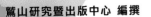耳朵聆聽，腳輕輕慢慢地提起，往前，放下，知覺清楚。

鷲山研究暨出版中心 編撰

# 禪

## 目錄

# Table of Contents

禪

## 編者說明

　　除了最常見的打坐，行禪也是一種禪修的途徑。因為容易嘗試，而且又不像坐禪那樣令人腳痛難耐，行禪一直是靈鷲山佛教教團致力推廣的禪修方法，也是靈鷲山無生道場舉辦雲水禪、企業禪、青年禪與兒童禪等各類禪修體驗課程必會安排的內容。

本手冊收錄靈鷲山開山和尚　上心下道禪師對行禪的意義、準備與步驟等修持重點的開示，祈願讓更多有志禪修者能夠掌握行禪的要領，循此躬身實踐，終能從中明心見性。

靈鷲山研究暨出版中心

## 行禪的意義

禪修不一定要盤著腿打坐，只要脊椎打直，
任何地方、任何時間都可以進行。坐在椅子上可以
做，躺著也可以做，什麼姿態都可以做。因此不只
有坐禪，行禪也是較易開悟的修行方法之一。在
《清淨道論》〈十種觀染〉中，有提到一位具有神
通力的凡夫長老，由於尚未證悟，故仍存恐懼，後
經證悟者的教導，進行行禪的練習，在走到第三步

的時候，就證悟阿羅漢果了。可見行禪是種非常好的禪修方式。

行禪，又稱為經行、動中禪。現今南傳佛教中，緬甸馬哈希禪師、泰國隆波田禪師，都曾依據《清淨道論》來大力提倡行禪。在北傳佛教中，自古也有專門以行走作為修行方式的般舟三昧，以及半行半坐方式的法華三昧、方等三昧等相關法門。而禪宗，更是重視此一修法，在坐禪的修行之外，也藉由行禪，也就是動中禪來輔助修行，以達到開悟的境界。

　　行禪的場地不一定要很寬敞，重要的是我們要感覺自己的行走。因為行禪是一個覺明的工作，要覺知腳的移動、覺知走路的步伐，也要覺知這個「行」，清清楚楚地知道自己在走，慢慢、緩緩地走。知道自己腳步起來，又慢慢放下去；起來，又慢慢下去，清清楚楚地覺知，也覺知到肚子裡的

「氣」的活動，肚子的上下，跟腳步一樣，一步一步慢慢地行。如此才能愈做愈清爽、愈做愈明朗，調劑了心的明度，腦筋也才會愈走愈清明、雜念愈少、妄想愈少。

# 行禪的操作口訣

耳朵聆聽，腳輕輕慢慢地提起，往前，放下，知覺清楚。

# 行禪開始前的身心準備

　　任何禪修法門的重點都不在姿勢，但是卻不能不注意脊椎的姿勢。行禪前，一定要先將脊椎打直，然後頭頂天、下顎微收，並將雙肩微微向內收攏。胸部與肩膀要像老鷹收覆翅膀的姿勢，兩肩稍微往內收斂。不要刻意把胸部挺得鼓鼓的，否則會讓胸腔脹得緊繃，容易產生胸悶或胸痛的狀況。由於脊椎掌管的是整個神經系統，從尾椎開始拉直到頭頂，才會享受到神經系統給予的安定感和舒暢感，也才會享受到禪修真正的放鬆與喜悅。

　　接著進行調息，做三至七次的深呼吸，讓呼吸舒暢。吸氣的時候要先將注意力放在脖子，下顎下壓，將喉嚨張開。雖然是用鼻子吸氣，但是我們要感覺自己正用喉嚨吸氣。讓氣從丹田、肚臍一路吸上來，到心，再到喉嚨，這樣輕輕鬆鬆地吸上來。如果覺得自己的肚子變大，而且吸得非常順暢，一口氣可以吸得很長，就是正確的吸氣；相反地，如果覺得自己吸得非常用力而且短促，就是沒有做對吐納的方法。吐氣的時候，則用鼻子輕輕鬆鬆地將氣給呼出去。呼吸，要深深地吸、慢慢地吐，不是用嘴巴吸氣，也不要用嘴巴吐氣。享受吸氣的快樂與呼氣的輕鬆──快快樂樂地吸氣，快快樂樂地吐氣，才是深呼吸。

接著，為了讓我們的心能夠安定而不攀緣，眼睛往下看，收攝眼根，同時也將我們的心往下沉，清楚感覺自己身體當下的「站立」。然後把雙手放到背後，肩膀放鬆自然下垂。手肘打直，用左手握住右手或右手握住左手都可以，或是將雙手交疊貼放於腹部。讓自己放鬆、放下，安靜下來，靜靜地聽、安靜地聽。

　　基本上，上述這些準備原則與九分禪的原理是相通的，若是大家熟悉九分禪，再來練習行禪，這是有相輔相成的好處的。九分禪是坐的姿勢，行禪則有行的姿勢，以及住(站立)的姿勢，大家可以細心地去體會。

# 行禪的動作解析

## 行進的方式(總說)

　　行禪，要用心去關注腳的每一個動作，在每一個動作裡，仔細觀察自己。因此在行禪時，我們先要站穩，站得很穩很穩，覺得已經沒有問題了，身體才往前傾。接著慢慢覺得腳後跟可以提起，才慢慢地開始動作。而且一次行禪最好走半個小時以上，用每一步去感受，讓每一步都有覺知。特別是不曉得如何拿捏自己覺性的初學者，更應該慢慢感受，太快就會模糊。（編按：覺性就是不生不滅、不會消失、遍滿虛空宇宙、不來去、離相的無為心。）

行禪一共有三個動作，就是腳的提起、往前和放下，但是在這三個簡單的動作裡，卻有許多不簡單的細微變化，那正是心的變化。

## 提起

行禪時，最重要的是把注意力放在所有動作上。腳部往前的時候，就要把心放在腳的動作上，不要分心去管其他的動作，就只要關注腳的提起。

如果腳跟已經提起來但自己卻沒有覺知到，那就是錯的！我們必須先感覺：「我要將腳提起來。」但是在這個時候，腳還不該提起來，而要繼續覺知：「我要開始了！」腳才開始提起。因為通

常我們不知道自己究竟是屬於身體，還是屬於那個
感覺，所以，覺知的目的是讓我們清楚自己的每個
觀念，也就是加強對自己的了解。

| 行進的方式 | 1.提起 | 2.往前 | 3.放下 |

## 往前

　　腳步往前的時候，不是像一般走路那樣跨步，而是要用關節把腳給提起來。注意力要放在腳上，將腳打平了，再往前推，把身體的重心提起來，慢慢地往前推進。

　　推前時，腳步不要跨得太大，跨出去的一腳腳跟與還沒移動的另一腳腳尖之間的距離，大約是一個腳掌的大小，較易保持身體的平穩。跨得太遠或太近，都可能失去平衡。

## 放下

　　向前推進之後，接著是把腳尖慢慢放下，然後腳跟也慢慢接觸地面。

　　當我們將腳放下時，要把心放在腳底，專心感受腳掌接觸地面的感覺，全程關注離開地面與接觸地面的感覺，體會那種踏實著地的感覺，然後保持靜止不動。

## 轉彎的方式

　　轉彎的方式有四個步驟，依序是：提起、側提、側放、轉身。

　　與行進的時候一樣，轉彎時也必須將注意力專心放在「轉」的念頭與動作上。這也要慢慢地進行，行禪的每一個動作都是慢的，盡量緩緩沒有關係。站好之後，慢慢地轉；再站好之後，才緩緩地開始下一步。

　　我們行進到某一處，準備停下來的時候，也要先告訴自己：「我要停下來。」才將自己的腳步緩緩地停下。轉彎之前，也要確定自己已經站得很穩了，才開始左轉或右轉。無論轉向左邊或右邊，或是轉向正後方繼續走，都要先靜靜地站著，覺知自己的動作，接著才開始進行提起、側提、側放與轉身的動作。

**轉彎的方式**　　1.提起　　　　　2.側提

3.側放　　　　　4.轉身

# 行禪的修持重點

　　主要我們還是配合九分禪的修行要點，來說明行禪時需要注意的地方。只是將靜態的坐姿轉變、延伸到動態的活動當中，同樣地去注意、去聆聽行禪時的寂靜，藉以培養我們的覺知力、持明力。

## 放鬆

把耳朵放鬆、頭部放鬆、肩膀放鬆,把全身都放鬆。將一切的罣礙都放下,也讓心胸鬆弛,讓每一個細胞都感覺非常的輕鬆、柔軟。

慢

　　禪修的功夫說穿了就是輕和慢的功夫，我們用禪調柔自己的心、調伏自己的心，也把粗魯的心變得細柔，讓自己隨時隨地保持心念的溫和，因此禪修的人對待一切事物都應該輕輕慢慢的，行禪也是這樣。輕輕的、慢慢的，就表示自己的心不粗。粗魯是一種衝動，動作愈急忙、愈粗魯，就愈沒有辦法感受寧靜。所以行禪的修持重點在於慢——把動作放慢，我們才會寧靜、才會安定。

行
禪

## 聆聽走的聲音

禪可以讓我們減輕壓力、放鬆身心,讓心神安定。只要安靜下來,心平安,一切也就跟著平安。所以行禪的時候不要講話,靜靜地走,靜靜地用耳朵去聆聽每一個動作——腳提起、往前、放下,聆聽寂靜,聆聽「行」的聲音。

我們的心,安靜的時候就會安定,不安靜就不會安定。安靜是一切萬有的本質,本來就具足的。我們所要聆聽的寂靜,就是這個最原始的無聲之聲。

## 覺知

　　行禪的時候要讓心專注於「覺知」——提起、往前與放下，每一個動作都要知覺清楚、聆聽清楚，我們的心才會安住在明朗。

　　如果覺知沒有走在前面，就會缺乏感受而感覺散亂。因此，行禪過程中不要讓意識迷迷糊糊、含糊籠統的。除了腳的動作，也不要忘記時時注意自己的呼吸，清楚地覺知吐納的起伏，甚至連妄念起來的時候也要覺知它、昏沉起來的時候也要覺知它、懈怠起來的時候也要覺知它。覺知就是讓我們在生活中察覺自己的念頭，掌握自己的行為，以般若空性的智慧，照破一切無明，遠離一切惡行。

## 止觀

　　行禪的每一個動作都是重要而且不可忽視的。「止」到哪裡，「觀」就跟著到哪裡。「止」在提起、往前與放下，「觀」也在提起、往前與放下。修持行禪法門，如果有足夠的定力，也能夠修得正覺，佛陀的弟子阿難尊者就是在躺臥下來的那一刻證得阿羅漢果，所以只要我們去做，將心攝在這裡、止在這裡、觀在這裡，就會有結果。（編按：「止」就是把心收攝在一境上；「觀」就是清楚明白的注意力。）

## 靜心安定

行禪的每一步都要輕輕地提起來,慢慢地往前,再輕輕地放下來。剛開始走的時候可能會站不穩,感覺快要跌倒,其實,真正不平衡的往往不是身體,而是我們的心,所以如果能將心平靜下來,就不會一直感覺搖搖晃晃的,心安定了,就會走得平穩。

行禪過程中能夠感受寧靜與安定，並覺知自己正在走路，才是最重要的。至於行禪的方向則沒有限制，只要我們的心靈往寧靜的地方走，行禪便會讓禪修者更容易認清自己。

# 結語─行，調心

　　我們會有煩惱，正是因為心神尚未調伏；只要心調伏了，我們就會很快樂。所以我們要有耐性，從緩慢的行禪開始練習。因為慢，讓一切從粗到細、從細到寧靜，最後能發現自己靈性的本質。所以行禪很容易就能讓心的散漫、妄想和不平衡沉澱下來。

　　行禪一步一步，就是覺知著自己正在走路，它可以讓自己離開妄想，專心地察覺自己的覺性。所以行禪的每一步都須仔細注意，每一個動作的感覺都要非常清楚，心才會寧靜、安定。覺知是為了讓我們明白自己並不是這個「身體」，只要我們踏踏實實地去做，就會發現這個身體並不是「我」，覺性才是「真我」。如果不持續地修行，覺性是很難發現的，所以要不斷地禪修，才會看見真我、找到佛。

持續不懈地修持，等到可以隨時隨地覺知腳的動作以後，平常走路時的每一個腳步、每一個動作，也都會覺得是一件很享受的事情──每一步都感覺到自己內在的靈性、都跟自己的靈性在一起，每一個腳步也都能踏到自己的靈性。

　　禪就是心，禪修也就是一個調整身心靈健康的法門。我們的心是一個很大的煩惱，它以躁動不安的頻率跳著，而禪修就是為了調伏我們躁動又煩惱的心，把它波動的頻率平緩下來，變成一潭明亮澄澈的止水，在眾多禪修的方法中，行禪就是其一。

　　如果腦筋總是亂轉，心的敏銳度就會降低，想要保持睿智，就要精進地禪修，讓自己的腦筋能夠在忙亂中得到休息和自由。天天禪修，排除矇蔽心燈的「無明障礙」，我們的心就會漸漸明亮起來，像光明燈一樣，天天亮著。

# Walking Meditation

Ears wide open, I slowly lift my foot; gently moving forward, I place it on the ground, fully aware all the while.

Research and Publication Center
of Ling Jiou Mountain

# Editor's Introduction

In addition to sitting meditation, walking meditation is also a commonly used practice in Buddhism. Because it's easier to learn and not as hard on the legs as sitting meditation, walking meditation is an important part of all the meditation courses taught at Ling Jiou Mountain.

This handbook presents the main points of walking meditation, in the form of excerpts from the oral teachings of Master Hsin Tao, the founder of Ling Jiou Mountain. All footnotes have been added by the editor. It is hoped that it will make clear the gist of the practice and prove to be of benefit to all those treading the path of awakening.

Research and Publication Center
of Ling Jiou Mountain

# The value of walking meditation

Practicing meditation doesn't necessarily mean that you have to sit down and cross your legs. As long as your back is straight, you can meditate at any time or place—so you can practice meditation while sitting in a chair or even while lying down. Like sitting meditation, walking meditation brings excellent results. In the Buddhist texts there is a story about a senior monk who had psychic powers, but had yet to attain liberation, as a result of which he was troubled by fear. Then an enlightened fellow monk instructed him in the practice of walking meditation, and after taking just three steps he became an arhat, an enlightened saint. This goes to show that walking meditation is a highly effective practice.

Also known as "moving meditation," walking meditation is given much emphasis in the meditation systems of such noted Theravada teachers as Mahasi Sayadaw of Burma and Luangpor Teean of Thailand. Walking meditation also plays a key role in Mahayana Buddhism, especially in such practices as "the meditation in which the buddhas of the present stand before one," the "dharma-flower absorption," and the "vaipulya absorption." Walking meditation is especially important in the Chan school, where it serves as an essential supplement to sitting meditation.

Walking meditation doesn't require a lot of space; the important thing is that you are fully aware of your movements. You have to remain completely mindful of the movement of your legs, fully attentive to each step. You also have to be clearly aware that you are walking, walking slowly and mindfully. You are aware as you lift up your foot, and as you place it down; lifting and slowly placing, all the while clearly comprehending your movements. Also be aware of the movement of the qi (vital energy) in your abdomen; your abdomen should be in step with your movements. This way, you feel increasingly refreshed, your mind becomes increasingly bright, and your desultory ideas and stray thoughts become increasingly less.

# A practice formula

Ears wide open, I slowly lift my foot; gently moving forward, I place it on the ground, fully aware all the while.

# Physical preparation

Whatever form of meditation you are practicing, it's essential to keep your back straight. Before you begin walking meditation, make sure that your back is straight; then keep your head up, slightly lower your jaw, and bring your shoulders slightly inwards. Your chest and shoulders should be like an eagle drawing in its wings. Don't make your chest bulge out; sticking your chest out distends the rig cage, and this tends to create tension or pain in the chest area. The spinal column is the central element of the entire nervous system, so you have to keep it straight and unobstructed, from the bottom of the spine all the way to the top of the head. Keeping your back and spinal column straight calms and stabilizes the nervous system, and this makes it possible to experience the peace and joy of meditation.

Now harmonize your breathing. Take between three and seven deep breaths, so that your breathing becomes smooth and comfortable. While doing this, first place your attention on your neck; then lower your jaw and open your throat. Although the air comes in through your nose, you want to feel as though you are breathing with your throat. Move the air from the lower abdomen to the navel, then to the heart and all the up to the throat. Breathe and relax; when your abdomen expands and each breath is quite long and smooth, then you know you've got it right. However, if it feels as though your breathing is short and forced, then you aren't breathing properly. In this case, use your nose to gently exhale. While breathing, you want to inhale deeply, and exhale slowly; don't use your mouth to breathe in, nor to breathe out. Experience joy as you breathe in, and tranquility as you breathe out; breathing in and out with happiness, your breath becomes deeper.

Next, in order to avoid distractions, keep your gaze downwards. Reining in the eye faculty helps to settle the mind. Clearly perceive the position of your body, then put your hands behind your back, allowing your shoulders to relax and drop down. Keeping your arms straight, use one hand to hold the other. Alternatively, you can place your hands on your abdomen, with your fingers interlaced. Relax, let go, calm down, and quietly listen.

These preparations are basically the same as those used for nine-minute meditation, which is practiced sitting down. The main difference is the posture. So if you are already familiar with the nine-minute meditation practice, then you will find that it goes well with walking meditation. It is also possible to practice meditation in a standing posture; feel free to try it out for yourself.

# How to practice

## How to walk

In practicing walking meditation, you have to attentively observe every movement of your legs; you have to closely observe yourself as you move. First, stand firmly in place; once you feel that your stance is firm and steady, then lean forward. Next, begin to move by lifting up one heel. It's best to continue walking for at least half an hour, fully aware of each step the whole time. Especially at the beginning, when you still don't have a feel for your awakened nature[1], it's important to go slowly, so that you gradually get attuned to the practice; if your movements are too fast it's hard to follow them in detail.

The actual walking practice consists of three movements: lifting, moving, and placing. However, within these three simple actions there are a lot of minute and complex movements going on; these are what you need to be aware of.

1.This refers to the unconditioned mind, which neither arises nor ceases, is all pervasive, and neither comes nor goes.

## Lifting up

In walking meditation, the most important thing is to pay close attention to every movement. As you move your leg forward, you place your entire attention on the movement of your leg, without bothering to notice any other movement.

If you lift up your heel, but you aren't fully aware while doing so, then you aren't practicing correctly. Normally, you begin by telling yourself "Now I'm going to lift up my foot." But in this case, first tell yourself "Now I'm going to begin," and only then start to lift your foot. Most of the time we are rather unclear about the state of the body and how we are feeling. This is why we need to cultivate the faculty of awareness.

How to walk    1.Lifting up      2.Moving forward      3.Placing down

# Moving forward

While moving forward, it's not like taking a normal stride; rather, you use your joints to lift the leg. Keep your attention on your legs. Once you place your foot flat on the ground, then start moving the other foot forward, lifting up the body's center of gravity, and slowly moving forward.

While moving forward, don't take long strides. Place your foot down about one sole's length in front of the other foot; this makes it easier to keep your balance. If your steps are too long or too short, you might lose your balance.

## Placing down

After moving forward, first touch the ground with the tip of your foot, and then slowly bring down your heel.

While bringing your foot down, place your attention on the sole of the foot; clearly note the feeling as your sole comes into contact with the ground. Be fully aware of the feeling as your foot leaves the ground, and as it touches the ground. Experience the solidity of the earth, and then remain motionless.

# Turning around

Turning around consists of four phases: lifting one foot, turning it to one side, placing it down, and repositioning the body.

As with moving forward, while turning you keep your entire attention on the idea and the action of turning. Turning is also done slowly; in walking meditation, every movement is done slowly, as slow as you like. Once you've come to the end of your walking space, stand still, and then slowly turn. Once you've fully turned around, stand still again for a moment before proceeding to walk.

Once you reach the end of your walking space, you get ready to stop by telling yourself "Now it's time to stop," then you slowly come to a complete stop. Before turning, first make sure that your standing posture is firm and stable, and only then begin turning to the left or right, as you like. The important thing is that you stand firm and still, with full awareness, before turning, and before starting to walk again.

Turning around

1.lifting one foot

2.turning it to one side

3.placing it down

4.repositioning the body

# The main points

The main points of walking meditation are the same as those for nine-minute meditation. It's essentially the same practice, but it's done in a moving posture rather than a stationary posture. Both use focused attention and listening to the sound of silence to strengthen your awareness and your faculty of perception.

## Relaxation

Relax your ears, relax your head, relax your shoulders, relax your entire body. Relax the mind, letting go of all worries. Relax to the point that every cell in your body becomes light and flexible.

## Slow movement

Whatever type of meditation you are practicing, it's important to make your movements slow and gentle. Meditation makes the mind more supple and pliable; it's a way of refining the coarse mind so that it becomes gentle in all situations. So whatever kind of meditation you are practicing, do everything gently and slowly; this is how you refine your mind. Coarse or rough movement is an expression of an impulsive mind; rushed and hurried movement makes the mind coarse and agitated. That's why in walking meditation you move slowly; moving slowly helps you calm down and experience peace.

# Listening

Meditation is an effective way to reduce stress; it helps you relax in body and mind. As soon as the mind calms down, everything becomes peaceful. So when practicing walking meditation, don't talk to anybody; just quietly walk, and quietly listen to the sound of all your movements—lifting, moving forward, placing—and listen to the sound of silence; listen to the sound of walking.

When the mind is quiet, it's peaceful; when it's not quiet it's not peaceful. Quiescence is the inherent quality of all things. This is the sound of silence, the primordial sound of silence that we want to listen to.

## Awareness

While practicing walking meditation you want to remain clearly aware as you lift your leg, move it forward, and place it down. With every movement, remain completely aware and attentively listen; this makes the mind settled and bright.

You have to walk together with your awareness; otherwise you can't follow your movements. So while practicing walking meditation, don't let your mind become muddled and vague. In addition to the movement of your legs, you also want to remain aware of your breath coming in and going out. As you progress in the practice, it becomes possible to be aware of stray thoughts as they arise; you can even reach a point where you are aware of drowsiness or slothfulness as they arise. So as your awareness becomes more developed, even in daily life you are aware of thoughts as they arise, giving you a greater degree of self-control. Eventually, you learn how to use the wisdom of emptiness to dispel all delusion, all the confusion which leads to unskillful actions.

# Stopping and observing[1]

In walking meditation every movement is important; don't overlook even the slightest movement. Wherever you stop your mind, that's where your observation is. When you stop your mind on lifting, moving, or placing, you are also observing lifting, moving, or placing. If your power of concentration is developed to a high degree, walking meditation can take you all the way to full awakening. For example, the Buddha's attendant Ananda attained arhatship just as he began to lie down. So if you rein in the mind, place it on its object, and observe, you are bound to get good results.

1. "Stopping" means fixing your attention on a particular object; "observing" means contemplating the object with complete lucidity of mind. Also rendered as "tranquility and insight."

## The tranquil mind

With every step you take in walking meditation, you gently lift up, slowly move forward, and gently place down. When you first learn this practice, you may feel a bit unbalanced, as if you are about to fall over. Actually, when this happens it's the mind that's out of balance, not the body. So when your mind is smooth and tranquil, then you won't feel as though you are staggering; the calmer the mind, the more stable the gait.

While practicing walking meditation, it's important to remain calm and at ease, all the while fully aware that you are walking. You can walk in any direction at all. The main thing is that the practice makes the mind more peaceful, for inner peace is the essential condition for self-awareness.

# Conclusion-Walking with a harmonious mind

The reason afflicted mental states arise is because the mind is agitated and out of control; as soon as you soothe the mind it calms down and happiness arises. This requires patience, and this is one of the things you learn in walking meditation. By slowing down, the coarse becomes refined, the refined becomes peaceful, and inner peace eventually culminates in insight into your original nature. So walking meditation is a highly effective way to settle down the scattered, distracted mind.

With each step, you are fully aware that you are walking; this helps you become free of stray thoughts so that you can perceive your awakened nature. This is why you have to pay close attention to every step; when you are clearly aware of every movement, the mind becomes peaceful. Through the cultivation of awareness, you come to realize that you are not the body; by practicing steadily and diligently, you come to understand that your true nature is the nature of awakening itself. In order to realize this, you have to maintain the continuity of the practice; this is how to find your true self, how to find the Buddha.

Keep practicing diligently until you get to the point where you are continually aware of the movement of your legs; afterwards you will find that every step you take, every movement you make, is a joyful experience. With every step you take, you feel as though you are in step with your essential nature. Every step takes you closer to your spiritual nature.

Meditation is the way of the heart; it's a way to become healthier in body, mind, and spirit. The undisciplined mind is the source of all sorts of trouble and tribulation. That's why we use meditation to pacify and train the restless mind. With steadfast practice, you eventually get to the point where the mind becomes as settled and clear as a limpid pool of water.

If your thoughts are always spinning around chaotically, then your awareness won't be very sharp. If you want to cultivate wisdom, then you have to use meditation practice to discipline the chaotic mind; then, even amidst the hustle and bustle of daily life, you get a rest and perhaps even a taste of freedom. With daily practice, you gradually eliminate all that obstructs your inherent wisdom, so that the mind becomes progressively brighter, like a brilliant lamp.

# Walking meditation

# Walking meditation

# Walking meditation

# Walking meditation

# Walking meditation

# Walking meditation

# Walking meditation

# Walking meditation

# Walking meditation

# Walking meditation

# Walking meditation

# Walking meditation

# Walking meditation

# Walking meditation

# Walking meditation

# Walking meditation

# Walking meditation

# Walking meditation

# Walking meditation

# Walking meditation

《禪修筆記系列 03》

**行禪**

導　　師：釋心道禪師

總 策 劃：釋了意
編　　撰：靈鷲山研究暨出版中心
主　　編：洪淑妍
責任編輯：李慧琳
美術編輯：宋明展
譯　　者：甘修慧

發 行 人：歐陽慕親
出版發行：財團法人靈鷲山般若文教基金會附設出版社
地　　址：23444新北市永和區保生路2號21樓
電　　話：(02)2232-1008
傳　　真：(02)2232-1010
網　　址：www.093books.com.tw
讀者信箱：books@ljm.org.tw

法律顧問：永然聯合法律事務所
印　　刷：國宣印刷有限公司
初版一刷：2012年12月
定　　價：250元
I S B N：978-986-6324-44-4

版權所有‧請勿翻印　　本書若有缺損，請寄回更換

《Meditation Notes Series, Number 03》

# **Walking Meditation**

Guiding teacher：Master Hsin Tao

Overall design：Shi Liaoyi
Producer：Research and Publication Center of Ling Jiou Mountain
Chief editor：Hong Shuyan
Executive editor：Li Huilin
Art editor：Song Mingzhan
English translation：Ken Kraynak

Publisher：Ouyang, Muqin
Distributer：Prajñā Cultural Foundation of Ling Jiou Mountain
Address：No. 2, Floor 21, Baosheng Road, Yonghe District, New Taipei City, 23444
Telephone：(02)2232-1008
Fax：(02)2232-1010
Website ：www.093books.com.tw
Comments：books@ljm.org.tw

Legal consultant：Perennial Group Law Firm
Printer：Golden Sun Printing
First edition：December, 2012
List price：NT$250
I S B N：978-986-6324-44-4

All rights reserved · Unauthorized copying and reproduction is prohibited.
If this book is found to be defective in any way, please send it to the distributer for
free replacement.

國家圖書館出版品預行編目（CIP）資料

行禪 / 靈鷲山研究暨出版中心編撰 -- 初版 --
新北市：靈鷲山般若出版，2012.12
面；公分 --（禪修筆記系列；3）
ISBN 978-986-6324-44-4（平裝）
1.佛教修持 2.佛教說法
225.87                     101026682